Money Whiz tm

Edition 8.2

Copyright 2002 – 2018 Geof Alex

Money Whiz tm is a publication on the different ways of accumulating financial success. It explains in an easy to understand format the various ways and methods of investing in shares and property. Shares can be the best investment for gaining wealth and Money Whiz tm covers how to make money in both the short or long term. It is designed for the professional or first time investor and helps you determine which method(s) of investment would best suit you. It also shows you how to use diversification to keep money safe as well as growing. It shows you how it is possible to earn a good living through shares, the advantages and traps of negative gearing shares and property and how to maximise benefits and investments when retired. The publication also covers property, superannuation, managed funds, running a business and budgeting. Very few become wealthy by relying solely on advisers and/or brokers. You must learn how to acquire the knowledge and confidence to make your own investment decisions.

ISBN 978-1-312-10116-6

A few of the topics covered by this publication are as follows:

- The share market	- Time in the market
- Percentage of profit to time	- Public floats
- Selling or buy orders	- Methods for selecting shares
- Performance example	- Negative gearing shares
- Discounts	- Managed funds
- Auto-stock loss	- Time and risk
- Blue chip shares	- Investing in property
- Chess system	- Negatively gearing property
- Diversification	- Positive gearing
- Quick profits	- Neutral gearing
- Spare cash	- Property loans
- Dividends	- Mortgage offset account
- Dividend reinvest	- Home you live in
- Formulas	- Crypto currency
- Market capitalisation	- Block chain technology
- P/E ratio	- Budgeting
- NTA	- Superannuation
- Bull and bear	- Annuities or pensions
- Compounding interest	- Turnover income and profit
- Paying out loans	- Tax rate
- Five reasons for investing in shares	- Reducing tax
- Researching	- GST tax
- Ten tips	- Wills
- Mining companies	- Power of attorney
- Don't speculate	- Share Whiz™

SHARE MASTER ™

☺

Shares are one of the best investments for gaining wealth. The Share Master (tm) publication explains the various ways of investing in shares to achieve your goals. It explains these methods in an easy to understand way and also the different reasons for using each method and how to determine which method(s) would best suit you. It also covers how to make money in the short or long term. Very few become wealthy by relying solely on advisers and/or brokers. You must learn how to acquire the knowledge and confidence to make your own investing decisions.

Share Master is a DIY investment guide.   C 2002 - 2018 G.Alex

1. Comparing the share market with other types of investments

The share market has always out performed all other investments over a longer period of time and has often had good short term results as well. It can also provide a regular income from interest paid (dividends) as well as investment growth. Most other investments only offer one or the other.

Shares are otherwise known as Equities or Stocks.

2. Brokers and fees

Discount brokers and full service brokers
To buy and sell shares you need to open an account with a brokerage firm. There are two types of brokerage firms. One is a discount broker. They buy and sell shares on your behalf without giving advice. The other type of brokerage firm charges more, but they will give advice in return. There is usually no fee involved to open up an account with a brokerage firm. You can also arrange to have money automatically transferred to and from one of your bank accounts to your broker when buying and selling shares.

Brokerage fees in respect to the size of purchase.
Fees charged by brokers to buy and sell shares can vary. For example a fee charged by a discount broker maybe the greater of the two options - $50 or 1% of the amount purchased per company plus around 0.15% tax.

Because of these fees, when you buy shares it would be better to purchase amounts close to $5000 as 1% of $5000 is $50. If only $1000 worth was purchased you would be required to pay the $50 fee which is then 5% of the $1000. If the shares in the company purchased rose 13% in a year and were bought and sold in that year, the $1000 parcel of shares would have cost 10% to buy and sell leaving a profit of just 3%. The $5000 parcel of shares however would have cost 2% to buy and sell leaving a healthier profit of 11%. Over a few years the differences are not as great. For example in four years the 13% gain would become 52%, less the 2% in fees for the $5000 purchase, leaving 50% compared to the 10% less in fees for the $1000 purchase which leaves 42%.

In public floats where there are no fees charged to buy the shares, smaller purchases are more profitable in a shorter period of time.

Name: always write down the name of the person whom you are dealing with and use it. Keep it for future reference, including phone dealings, speak politely and courteously.

3. Share price importance

It is not important if the share price is 50 cents or $10.00 as you may buy $3,000 of either and it is not the number of shares you are buying that is important but the growth potential of the company and/or share price.

Eg 6000 shares at 50 cents = $3,000 or 300 share at $10.00 = $3,000. Both rise in price 22% you now have 6000 shares at 61 cents = $3660 or 300 shares at $12.20 = $3660.

4. Percentage of profit to time

In two month's 10%, after fees, could be considered a good profit. Whereas 10% made in two years wouldn't be nearly as good. However other things may come into consideration eg the ongoing dividends payments and what is done with the proceeds if the shares are sold after two months. If the proceeds are not invested in as profitable shares, the money may have been better left which would have also saved you the buy and sell fees.

5. Selling or buy orders

When buying or selling a share you may instruct your broker to sell your shares when or if they reach a higher price. You may also instruct your broker to buy a share if it falls to a certain price. This order will usually stay on for 3 to 4 weeks unless a time period is requested.

Please note some **calculators** (possibly cheaper versions) may give incorrect answers. For example 2 + 5 x 2 = 12 however some calculators may give the answer 14. The rule is divisions and multiplications are calculated first. If the formula however was (2 + 5) x 2 then of course the answer would be 14. Keep this in mind when calculating.

6. Performance examples

30/7/2009 bought 151 Wesfarmers shares at $26.43 = $3990.93

$3990.93 + (Total Fee $45.40 + (GST 10% 4.54)) = $4040.87

13/6/2012 Sold 151 at $30.77 = $4646.27 + (Div = $873.71) = $5519.98

Profit: $5519.98 – 4040.87 = **$1479.11** or $1479.11 / $4040.87 = **36.6%**

11-2-05 bought 335 Alinta Limited shares at $8.95 = $2998.25

$2998.25 + (Total Fee $54.45 + (GST 10% 5.45)) = $3008.15

23-3-05 Sold 335 at $9.70 = $3249.50 + (Div = $129.20) = $3378.70

Profit: $3378.70 - $3008.15 = **$370.55** or $370.55 / $3008.15 = **12.32**%

25/6/96 bought 850 ANZ Bank shares at $5.86 = $4981

$4981 + (Total Fee $100 + (Tax 0.3% $17.94)) = $5098.94

1/5/97 Sold 850 at $8.19 = $6961.50 + (Div 5.64% = $336.76) = $7298.26

Profit: $7298.26 - $5098.94 = **$2199.32** or $2199.32 / $5098.94 = **43.13**%

1/8/95 bought 1600 Dunlop shares at $2.96 = $4736

$4736 + (Total Fee $100 + (Tax 0.3% $14.21)) = $4850.21

25/6/96 Sold 1600 at $2.93 = $4688 + (Div 7.60% = $359.94) = $5047.94

Profit: $5047.94 - $4850.21 = **$197.73** or $197.73 / $4850.21 = **4.08**%

25/6/96 bought 2800 Simeon Wine shares at $1.80 = $5040

$5040 + (Total Fee $100 + (Tax 0.3% $22.20)) = $5162.20

1/5/97 Sold 2800 at $3.10 = $8680 + (Div 4.59% = $339.66) = $9019.66

Profit: $9019.66 - $5162.20 = **$3857.46** or $3857.46 / $5162.20 = **74.73**%

5-4-04 bought 270 QBE shares at $11.19 = $3021.30

$3021.30 + (Total Fee $54.45 + (GST 10% 5.45)) = $3081.20

23-6-05 Sold 270 at $15.85 = $4279.50 + (Div = $104.15) = $4383.65

Profit: $4383.65 - $3081.20 = **$1302.45** or $1302.45 / $3081.20 = **42.27**%

Average: Buys $24767.48 + Fees $524.09 = Total in $25291.57

    Sold $32504.77 + Divs $2143.42 = Total out $34648.19

    Profit $34648.19 - $25291.57 = **$9356.62**

    or $9356.62 / $25291.57 = 0.3699 * 100 = **36.99%** profit

At the time you buy you have lost the brokerage fee and the share price may full before rising and this may take some time. It may be several years before you make a nice profit and there is no guarantee of making a profit. Shares are usually a long term investment, 4 years plus.

7. Discounts through the Internet and helpful tips

Some brokers give a discount when shares are bought on the Internet.

There are brokers who provide a free call number. By inquiring you may find some helpful and interesting tips. Remember though it has been known on some occasions for a tip to be given in order to help sell stocks for other customers. Some brokers also recommend companies that they have floated and they may not be very good.

8. Auto stock loss and profit setting

For a fee say $13.00 you can set an automatic sell price so if your shares fall to this designated price or slightly below they are then sold. Eg you buy 3000 shares at $1.00 each you set a 17.5% loss. This means if the price drops to $0.83 cents they are sold automatically or the same shares may have risen to $1.30 each you set your profit to 6%. This means if the price drops back to $1.06 cents they are automatically sold. (You also need to set a maximum price drops percentage so as if the price drops too quickly and falls to far below your sell price the sell is automatically cancelled.)

9. Blue chip shares

Blue chip shares are usually more secure as their assets and profits usually outweigh their debts.

10. The chess system

The CHESS system (Clearing House Electronic Subregister System). When opening an account it would be recommended that you apply to go on the chess system. There is no charge involved and this will enable you to sell your shares straight away without waiting for the appropriate paper work and share certificates. You should record your chess number HIN (Holder Identification Number) for use when purchasing shares.

11. Diversification

It maybe unwise to place all your money in one company or sector (Do not lock in) just in case they have a bad run. As your money grows it can be safer and therefore more profitable to spread your share portfolio over the different sectors such as banking and finance, telecommunications, health, retail, mining, tourism etc. Once you have a good selection you may like to double up on some of the better performing stocks you feel also have long term stability and potential.

12. Quick profits

A quick profit may be made in shares however they are usually a long term investment of one to four or more years. The share market has consistently out performed all other investments over a period of time and there are often good short term results as well.

Day Trading is a method you use to try and make quick profits, but only about 10% actually achieve this. Some of them are using complex computer programs that look at re-occurring patterns over a period of time and real time data from the internet (share market) to help determine what and when to buy and sell. If you are thinking of attempting day trading you would be advised to study the share market for a long time and perhaps use at least 8 months of simulated runs, using shares that also have a good long term potential.

{Have a long term strategy}

13. Avoiding panic
{Planning and Patience}

Over-reaction
The share market can tend to over react as people panic to buy or sell. Shares can rise far above their value or fall far below their value.

Falling share prices may also be accelerated by the Auto Stock Loss making them fall faster and further. Then maybe investors looking for good buys take advantage of some of the low prices and the market partly recovers.

Avoid panicking, however sometimes quick decisions are required. You should pre-plan what you are going to do if the share price rises above or below a certain price according to profit and time. If a company or sector has a bad report will you get out quick or ride it out? If a share price rises dramatically will you take a quick profit in case it falls back or is it possible the company may continue to perform well. You should try and avoid selling on a possible low or buying at a possible high. Remember do the research and that shares are mostly long term.

{All booms have a bust} In Shares and Property

{Buy on gloom, sell on boom}

Property
When the property market is booming the share market may be in decline. The property market may become over valued and the share market under valued some of which may be caused by panic and greed. You don't want to be caught and you don't want to miss out. Eventually however the markets will correct and or swap to an over valued share market and an under valued property market. Of course many other factors cause these booms and busts and you must be careful not to buy in the peak or sell out at the bottom. These things however can be hard to determine and we do not have the use of a crystal ball, but they are factors to be aware of and with patience and common sense may assist in a good profit. Some people believe there is a seven-year cycle (+-7?)

Property is more likely to follow the value change of other properties in the same area however a share price may not necessarily follow the average change in value of the share market. It may well under perform or over perform the average.

14. Spare cash in trust funds (high interest or internet accounts)

It is a good thing to leave a little money on hand in case an opportunity arises to buy shares in a company that suddenly becomes a good buy or appears promising. Most banks provide accounts that pay a reasonable interest rate and still provide access to your money, such as a Trust Account (high interest accounts) - eg minimum balance of $1000, additional deposits or withdrawals of amounts over $500 interest calculated daily and paid quarterly. Also internet online saving accounts can offer good interest with no minimum balance however you still need your normal savings account to transfer your money to and from the high interest accounts. If you have a percentage or a set amount of money you wish to keep aside in your trust account, that is not for shares (eg 25%), you should be careful that you do not become addicted to the share hype and over spend on the share market. You may sell your shares at any time but it may take about 2 weeks before your money is in your account.

(Note most bank accounts have fees, you therefore should only have the bare minimum number of bank accounts and always keep an eye on the fees).

14.5 Spare cash: Some people like to put away spare cash by buying coins eg special limited releases from the mint. Whilst some releases are done in too larger volumes to grow in value other releases are a little more limited and may well exceed the average interest rate growth in value. Some of the coins are proofs and made of gold or silver.

Also first and last edition notes sometimes go quite well, however some may of course only retain their face value you therefore may endure a loss due to the additional cost when purchasing the collectors kit. This is therefore an investment that requires a little research and caution before proceeding. One example, a proof coin released in 2004 commemorating the Ghan rail from Darwin to Adelaide which was made of silver with a face value of $5 sold from the mint boxed up including its limited edition paperwork details for $68.50. On a day in Feb 2006 a seller on eBay was trying to sell one of these coins for $175, another for $250 and one that was on auction, 5 minutes before auction end had reached $120. This is a 75% increase in value, however there are no guarantees with this type of investment. It is just that the consumers are prepared to pay this amount for this particular $5 limited edition proof coin. In contrast a $1 coin released in 2005 to commemorate the WW2 peace that has been released into circulation will most likely always be valued at $1.

(Learn to save, reduce cost and sell unnecessary items especially those that cost money).

You could invent something and collect royalties, however this may be unlikely as even if you did invent something only 1 in 10 inventions get patented and only 1 in 10 of these make it to the market place and only 1 in 10 of these make a profit. You ideally need a lot of initial capital to afford the patents, prototypes and marketing.

There are also some inventions that do make a profit, but not by the owner as patents were not sought or not sought in the right country. If you took the risk of not having a patent you may be able to enter into confidentiality agreements and licensing agreements with a company to manufacture and pay you a royalty particularly if it is an item that has a limited market and which may not be worthwhile somebody copying.

You could start a business, but usually you need enough funds to finance yourself for a year until you build up your customer base and start making a reasonable profit. You may also end up working fewer hours in the long run. It can sometimes be a matter of being in the right place at the right time, but consideration needs to be given to your knowledge base, business needs in the area and recognising niche markets. Statistically around 10 percent of businesses fail within the first year and after around 3 years 25 percent of businesses have failed. Some businesses may not actually provide you extra wealth, just extra working hours. Don't forget if you run a business you need adequate insurance.

Perhaps one of the best ways to make more money is to increase your skills so as to obtain a more secure, higher paid employment. As such it is often wise to take advantage of any courses or learning opportunities that you are able to participate in. This will most likely help with your resume and it may even be the course you thought initially had the least use or relevance that turns out to be something you can utilise in the future for obtaining a better paid or more satisfying occupation or lifestyle improvement.

If you are able to you can at times save money in the long run through initial planning and a small capital outlay eg instead of using a landline phone to make your calls, you could consider using VOIP voice over internet protocol, if you had internet, by purchasing a small VOIP adapter. For a small or monthly fee it is then possible through some providers to make all your local and long distance calls for free.

Adequate and quality insulation can considerably lower your heating and cooling costs over the long term. Efficient heating and cooling products such as an inverter heat pump also could provide a long term worthwhile saving. Possibilities to consider also include solar power particularly if you are able to obtain a solar system with some assistance from government grants etc. If the total cost to you was $6000 which in turn covers your total power costs on average say $2000 p/a this would equal about a 33% return on your investment which is 2000 / 6000 * 100 = 33.3 and you would also therefore recoup your costs after around 3 years. Even without rebates it's a worthwhile exercise to do the figures because it should be a good return on your initial investment.

A lot of successful people have accredited a part of their success to having an easy and effective job list. One list can be created for long term jobs, things to be done in a year or more, another for what needs to be done within a month or maybe a week and another for daily or half daily jobs. A job list could consist of things that need to be done, things that would like to be achieved, as well as goals. Although they are time dependent, time is not necessarily the most important consideration to be given when setting the order. When setting the order of the jobs they could be prioritised eg from A to D, with A being the jobs with the most priority and most urgency. It can then be decided which of the high priority / urgency jobs will be done first. It can sometimes be tempting to do the jobs that take the least amount of time or work first, but this could lead to jobs of priority and urgency not being completed in time which therefore could lead to missed opportunities which could also be the case if one operates without the use of some form of job list.

Remembering names is also something that is used by successful people and is generally also good manners. Successful people will often record the names of people as someone is more likely to assist you if you show that you think they are important enough for you to remember their name.

Remember if you need help you shouldn't be hesitant to ask because most people are only too happy to assist if they are able.

It is also useful to keep a diary as it can sometimes be an advantage to recall dates of events and some details of what occurred in the past.

It is also beneficial to have a good system for storing and easily locating important documents and receipts etc.

{it is perhaps being well organised that is also a useful tool for being successful}

15. Dividends:

A $10 Share that pays a dividend of $1 therefore has a dividend yield of 10% which is the price divided by the dividend paid $10.00 / $1.00 = 10%. Dividend yield is based on the last dividend paid by the company. For example if a share was worth $10 and a dividend of $1 or 10% is paid and then the share rises to $20 the dividend is still calculated on the last paid dividend which was $1 and which is now 5% of the $20 share. However if the company profits have also risen the next actual dividend paid may be $2 which is still 10%. If the company profits have fallen the dividend may have also fallen below 10%. Usually dividends remain reasonably proportional to share price.

Dividends and profit
Often shares pay a Dividend (Dividend Yield). The Dividend Yields may vary in percentage paid, payment periods and type. For example the percentage paid usually varies between 1% and 8%. They may be paid quarterly, half yearly or yearly. They may also be franked, partly franked or unfranked. Franked dividends are a credit that may be claimed on your tax. This credit can be more than you owe on your tax for the divided paid or less. If the franked credit is more than you owe on the dividend paid, the remaining credit can be used on other taxes owed or paid back as a refund.

For example a dividend published at 4.5% fully franked would indicate that another 30% of the amount paid to you in dollars has been paid as a tax credit which you may claim if you owe tax to reduce your tax owed or if you do not owe tax you can claim the credit back as a refund.

This means the total dividend, counting dividend paid 4.5% plus dividend credit 1.93% would equal 6.43%. (100% - 30% = 70%, 30% / 70% = 42.86%, 4.5% * 42.86% = 1.93%, 4.5% + 1.93% = 6.43%, 6.43% * 30% = 1.93%)

Under the GST if no amounts are owed on your Tax the franked credit will be refunded to you as in the past if you could not use the credit on tax owed the credit was lost. Companies may pay little or no dividends for three reasons. Firstly it can be because the company reinvests most of their profits into research and/or growth. A good example of this is with mining companies who continually explore new areas for more minerals. Secondly the shares are over priced because people like the company and are prepare to pay the higher prices ask by the sellers as dividends are partly calculated on profit as compared to price. A share price may rise a little just before the dividend is due to be paid. This is because buyers are entitled to the whole dividend even if they only purchase the shares the day before the payment is due. Like wise a share price may fall a little after the dividend has been paid. Thirdly it can be because the company is not making a good profit.

Dividend Reinvest
Dividends paid by a company can be taken as Dividend Reinvest which means your dividend payment is used to obtain more shares in the company with no brokerage fees and the shares are usually sold to you at a discount price. This should help your investment grow and so the dividend increases and so on. Shares given through Dividend reinvest are usually counted as income and therefore are taxed as income. Another option similar to dividend reinvest offered by some companies is the bonus option plan which operates in much the same way except the shares given may not be counted as income instead just increasing the total number of shares you own and may only be taxed when you sell them as Capital Gains Tax.

16. Company figures and formulas

Market Capitalisation (Rank) is the total number of shares issued multiplied by the last sale price of the company in Millions of Dollars. The top 300 companies are published weekly in order with number one being at the top of the ladder. If you bought the top 6 companies odds are you could make a good profit on average. A better way may be to research the companies for those rising the ladder the fastest and are in the top 170.

The **P/E ratio**, (price / earnings) is the current total value of the shares divided by the after-tax earnings of the company per year. Eg a company that has shares to the total value of $4,000,000 and earns $500,000 p.a. would have a P/E ratio of 8, which also means if the share is at $2 the company is earning 25 cents on each individual share or the number of years the company would take to earn its total share value. ($0.25 * 8 years = $2.00) Therefore the lower the P/E ratio the better, However This Can Be Almost Irrelevant as it does not take into consideration the growth possibilities of the company, the assets of the company, or the life expectancy of the company etc. The P/E ratios may vary between industry types. A good P/E ratio is usually below 20.

NTA = (Net Tangible Assets). Company assets $4,000,000 subtract debts $2,000,000 = $2,000,000 divided by the number of share 2000000 = 100 cents or $1.00 per share. To compare NTA, 100 cents divided by 100 and divided by the price of the share $2.00 = .5 or 50% this figure is easier to compare with other company figures. The higher the figure the better it is.

DTC (Dividend Times Covered) company after-tax Earnings Per Share (EPS) 25 cents divided by dividend paid per share 20 cents = 1.25. To compare DTC to other Company multiply the DTC 1.25 by the dividend yield percentage 10% = 12.5%. The Companies with the highest figures are the best.

Figures published in the papers are for the previous day's trade only.

Example: Buy $1.98, Sell $2.04, Last sale $2.00, Move +.03, (move of +.03 indicates the previous days last closing sale was $1.97) Volume traded * 100s 12000, Dividend Yield 10.00%, P/E ratio 8, NTA 100 per share in cents, Market Capitalisation 6,866 in $Millions or 18 in the ladder order.

The below formulas are often found in company prospectuses. Some of these formulas give a different result but mean virtually the same thing and are usually not very helpful because they need to be used in conjunction with other information eg growth potential and compared with other companies that are similar in size and industry etc.

EPS (Earnings Per Share) is calculated by dividing the Net Profit After Tax eg. $500,000 with the total number of ordinary shares eg. 2000000 which gives the EPS answer, in this case 25 cents. A Share price of $2.00 divided by its EPS 25 cent equals its P/E Ratio in this case 8.

DPS (Dividend Per Share) is calculated by dividing the total dividends paid eg. $400,000 with the total number of ordinary shares eg. 2000000 which gives the DPS answer, in this case 20 cents.

Debt Ratio (Liabilities / Assets) If a company's liabilities are $2,000,000 and its assets are $4,000,000 it Debt ratio is 0.5 There is no ideal figure, the figure will normally be less than one. An acceptable ratio is between 0.4 to 0.6. The lower the figure the better how ever a high level of debt caused by expanding companies (growth) could be an advantage.

Dividend Cover is calculated by dividing the EPS answer by the DPS answer eg. Using the examples above 25 / 20 which equals 1.25.

NPAT = (Net Profit After Tax) = Pre tax Profit - Tax Payable.

EBIT = (Earnings Before Interest & Tax)

EAI = (Estimated Annual Income).

Please note: That when these figures are published (PER, Div etc) they are based on the last actual calculated figures of the company and companies may only calculate their figures every 4 months. Therefore figures given in between are based on an estimated calculation of the current company share price and the last figures given by the company, so when the next company calculations are done the figures such as dividends may end up being a little higher or lower depending on company profits etc etc during that period.

17. The bull and bear market

Bull Market is one that is rising over the long term. A bull is a person who expects it to rise.

Bear Market is a market that is declining over the longer term. A bear is a person who expects the market to decline.

18. Good monopolies

Companies that have a **good monopoly** in their industry have usually been good long term performers.

19. Saving and compounding interest

Compounding

The sooner you begin to save the better eg if you saved $30 a week for 10 years at 7% interest compounding quarterly you would have $22,698.51 of which you have contributed $15,600.00. The last $30 earned 52 cents in interest and the first $30 has earned $31.10 in interest because of the compounding effect over time. The more money you can invest earlier the better the profits.

Shares can have an even bigger compound effect on your savings with the share price growing and by using dividend reinvest.

Using the 72 rule

If you received 4% interest compounding once a year it would take approximately 18 years to double your money {72 / 4 = 18} If you received 12% interest compounding once a year it would take approximately 6 years {72 / 12 = 6}. Don't forget the effects of tax and inflation of course.

{Saving is better than buying a bargain you may need some time in the future. Buy only what you need when you need it}

{What is the right balance of work and leisure, savings and luxuries?}

{How much money do you need to make you happy ☺ and how much money will you need to keep you happy? Plan and sacrifice a little for the future}

{The more you earn and/or the more you can live below your means, the more you can save}

{Improving your qualifications and or skills may help you earn more and therefore save more}

{Prepare your budget and look for any unnecessary or non-worthwhile expenses}

{You may be able to make some short term earnings by selling items you no longer need}

{Weigh up long term goals with expensive hobbies. eg electronic gizmos, the thousand of dollars CD collections, expensive sports, expensive to run vehicles, cigarettes/alcohol, DVD's, dining out. A moderation of pleasure and saving. Every dollar counts}

{Wealth = the more you earn, the less you spend and the amount you can invest. The more some earn the more they increase their expenses not their investments}

{Keep fit ☼, live below your means, save in moderation}

{The onlooker says your success is due to good luck not hard work and planning}

{You need to plan and suffer a little in order to build wealth}

{University graduates have been surveyed. 5% of them say they have written down their long term goals. 25 years later 85% of the 5% have reached their goals and 5% of the others that didn't write their goals down have achieved the success they had hoped for. }

You may not think doing a budget including a details of every cent you have spent during a period of say a month is necessary, just reduce your spending as much as possible. Pay off existing bills and save, however it is worthwhile doing a budget because you may be very surprised by the results. The accumulative effect of some little things you are buying may add up to quite a bit over a month. It's perhaps the unexpected things a budget finds that makes it a very worthwhile exercise. There are many things to make it hard to save eg if you are renting a T.V. it may be cheaper to buy in the long run but the rent payments make it harder to save for one. There are an increasing number of methods to milk your money and make it harder for you to get ahead, credit card interest, rent, unnecessary subscriptions, paid T.V. etc. and the new necessities of mobile phones, internet etc.

Price a new car then see what you could save on buying one that is around 18 months old.

It's also a good idea to have a reasonable amount of money allocated for savings in your budget as this money may also be needed for unexpected bills including costs which you may incur unnecessarily due to a third party giving you misleading misinformation which may have been done unintentionally or intentionally to allow them to unreasonably gain extra profits from you. Eg cost blow outs and scams. There is always someone out there that would like to keep you broke so as they can benefit or to help to keep the revenues flowing.

Contracts - Mobile phone, internet, pay TV etc. A well chosen contract may provide you with a cheap, convenient service. A bad contract may cost you a lot more than you were expecting with hidden fees or more frequent usage than you estimated and may also lock you in for a long time with hexy exit fees and penalties. It would be well advised and worthwhile to research contracts you are considering and other similar options provided by other companies. It would be worth your while to research a lot of companies to make sure you get the best priced deal to suit your circumstances. For mobile phones you may consider using prepaid where you pay before using the service eg you pay for $100 phone credit up front and when that expires you are not left owing any unexpected amount. What sounds the cheapest may end up being the most expensive in the long run so it pays to research thoroughly and avoid getting caught out. Often the claims of free bonuses have hidden expensive strings attached.

You have three goals all costing about the same, but only the money for one at the moment. Which would you choose to do first? 1) You would like to purchase a small recreational fishing boat, 2) A small portfolio of blue-chip shares with good growth potential that also pay a reasonable dividend and 3) some solar panels for your house or dwelling. You could chose the solar array first as you have calculated the return on savings on your power bill is equivalent to being paid 30% interest on the investment and the return savings on your power will then help you save the additional money for your other goals. Second choice may be the shares as the dividend return on these is say 5%, but as perhaps they are fully franked when you take the franking into consideration you may be earning around 8% as well as the growth on the shares. There is also the added ability if your situation changes and you need money for some unexpected expense you can liquidate or sell the shares.

Your third choice after the third two choices have helped you more quickly accumulate the finances to get your three goals achieved may be the small boat, remembering this will likely be an ongoing cost with registration, fuel and insurances etc. However you may decide life's enjoyments area little bit more important and you may also need access to your funds in case something unforseen happens so you may decide to go for the shares first, the boat second and the solar array last. From a financial sense though you are better off to deal with things that reduce your costs of living or increase your income first. Over time this could make the difference of earning you or saving you many thousands of dollars. Many people choose the small boat first and as this is the option that incurs ongoing running costs therefore may prevent the other goals being reached and or greatly increases the time it takes to achieve all goals.

Statistics suggest 93.5% of people will be dead or dead broke at age 65, 5% will be financially independent and 1.5% will be rich.

Statistics suggest that of those that win lotto many will be worse of in 3 to 7 years time.

Conclusion it is not as easy to manage money or maintain wealth as it may seem, plan and proceed with caution.

If all the world's wealth was spread equally each person would have around $3,000,000.

20. Paying out loans

Unless you can earn more interest from an investment than you are being charged on your **loan** you should pay the loan before investing.

You invest $2,000 at 6% you earn $120, your loans for $2,000 at 13% costs you $260. The $140 is your loss and the compounding effect over time would increase your losses. If you have a loan you should endeavour to pay it off as quickly as possible, (however it is a good idea to keep a little bit of money invested for emergencies).

It is always interesting to divide your payment amount by the total number of payments and subtract the amount borrowed to see the total interest you will pay. Due to the compounding effect and the usually high interest the amount can be a lot higher than the amount borrowed.

{One of the first steps in saving money is to reduce or eliminate loans}

{Money can't buy happiness but it helps a lot more than debts}

{A survey showed that some of the happiest people were those that were slightly more financially successful than their friends}

{Excess money can become a problem if you allow it to isolate you}

{Its therefore more important to make more friends than money, but money may help the latter or may hinder ☺}

{To increase wealth you may need to change your habits or take the first step and for some people change is almost impossible. Changes can be all for the positive, but in some circumstances change can have a certain amount of risk, how much risk are you prepared to take, have you a plan if things do not work out. You need to feel confident and understand your plan and be ready for the first step and change}

21. Five reasons for buying shares

It is sometimes said that there are **five reasons** for buying share.

One is income, a share paying a good high dividend of 6% or higher can credit this dividend into your bank account.

Second is growth which is obviously a company with good growth potential and possibly a dividend reinvest option.

Thirdly, a little of both, would be a company with reasonable growth potential and paying a dividend of around 4% which is being paid to you.

Fourth is a share that may rise quickly providing a fast profit?

Fifth is a share that steadily rises over a period of time providing good long-term growth?

A better way to achieve reason one **(income)** can be to pick a share mainly on its growth potential even if the dividend is smaller, have the dividend paid to you instead of using dividend reinvest. As the share price grows in value so do your dividend amounts. A share that costs $1 each and pays a 3% dividend and then rises to $3 per share still paying a 3% dividend is equivalent to receiving a 9% dividend on the original price of $1. Thus in the long term this provides you with a higher dollar dividend and the bonus of good capital growth.

If option four is desired (quick profits) a share that also has good long term growth potential should be chosen in case the short term goal is not realised. The opportunity for growth is the most important factor by far.

Current Dividend Paid 10% multiplied by current Share Price $4.00 divided by Share Price Paid $2.00 = Dividend Paid 20% if share price was still at price paid $2.00.

$$10\% * \$4.00 / \$2.00 = 20\%$$

22. Down turn in share markets and good dividends

{If patience is your game, not time then the odds are certainly in your favour}

{Those without patience assist those with patience in profiting}

In the event of the share market falling a quality blue chip share that shows a good potential for growth and also pays a good dividend of more than 4% can be a good investment. Because the price falls due to a down turn in general share market prices or confidence the dividend should rise accordingly. This makes it an even more attractive investment for other investors, thus usually preventing the price from falling too far.

23. Buying low priced shares

Sometimes a share with a low price, eg 50 cents, can be more likely to rise and fall a bigger percentage in a shorter space of time. A 5 cent rise may not seem much, and some people maybe more likely to pay an extra 5 cents for the share. This 5 cent increase is actually a 10% rise, whereas a $20 share that rises $1 has only risen 5% and a dollar is more noticeable.

24. Knowledge to make your own investment decisions

You can learn how to acquire the knowledge and confidence to make some of your own investing decisions, and not continually pay a percentage of your wealth to brokers and advisers. You must also learn when to act and when to have patience. However a good broker can be worth his weight in gold if he can be found and continually values your clientele.

25. Researching companies

When buying shares it is advisable to research the companies past growth in share prices, dividends, assets, profits, liabilities, P/E ratio, and **potential growth**. Magazines (such as Smart Investor, Financial Review and their website) or old newspapers can be used to obtain past prices and other facts. The Internet and Austext also display share prices with regular updates.

Some Brokers also provide information on the Internet including useful graphs etc. Share Buyers Clubs can also be good to join if one is available in your area. Talk to a few brokers. Be prepared to let time work for you.

26. Ten Tips ☺

1 Know and research the company.

2 Know the share price and dividend history.

3 Select a company with good growth potential. (Does the price graph show a good history of growth).

4 If possible select a company that's paying a reasonable dividend, franked or unfranked as suits.

5 Find out if the company has a good Market Capitalisation in the top 200, P/E ratio below 30 and has a good NTA, at least 20% of the share price.

6 Find out if the company has a good monopoly in its industry as this maybe worth considering.

7 Is the company a possible take over target?

8 A low priced share may also be an advantage if the above points 1, 2, 3, 5 are good.

9 Diversify your share portfolio, if finances allow, to keep money safe as well as growing whilst trying to keep brokerage fees at a low percentage.

10 {Check reports {Magazines, internet} and ask brokers what companies have a good growth potential and are reasonably non speculative (safe) etc. Timing the market isn't as important as time in the market}

27. Mining companies

Mining share prices can vary considerably depending on the price of metals. However a company with good assets, capital, low running costs and a long life expectancy who are still undergoing new exploration may be an excellent buy as a good mineral find may substantially increase their value.

28. Speculating

{Buy on rumour, sell on fact} or

{Don't speculate, if you want to accumulate}

Don't speculate. However if your research on the company shows that it has a good outlook (growth, profit) and there is a promising rumour that something big may happen, such as a take over bid or a new mineral find, you may have a good buy. If the price has not already risen too much you may find a quick profit remembering the price may also rise far over the value of the share and then fall off. If you buy and then sell at the right time you can make a quick profit. In cases like this it is a good idea not to be too greedy and predetermine the price (percentage of profit) you are going to sell at in relationship to time. Always leave a little profit for the next guy. If the share price falls you may also set a price to sell at (percentage of loss), if you think the price may not recover because of new information.

If you have made a quick profit be just as careful when reinvesting. Don't rush in as you may lose what profit you have made. It is alright to add to your cash on hand until you are totally satisfied in another share investment.

You may also follow the price of a company that has low debts and a good growth potential, but because it is in a market affected by other things such as mineral prices is not paying a high dividend or any dividend at all (as a company falling in price that has a high dividend makes the dividend rise which tends to stop the price of the share falling too much as the dividend becomes too attractive).

The price may tend to regularly fluctuate within a certain price range. You may be able to obtain the shares at the lower price and sell at the higher price making a reasonable profit each time.

You may also learn of a mining company, perhaps a new one that has just discovered a substantial and long lasting resource which greatly increases current resources. However as it may take some time for the company to reach production and start selling the price might only rise slowly for a while and it may take several years for the price to start dramatically changing. A company like this may be a good long term speculative buy.

If you decide to do a little speculating for short term profits determine what amount or percentage of your money you intend to speculate with and stick to this amount. Also remember when selecting such companies check that they also have good long term potential and a few sound figures in case the short term results you are hoping for do not eventuate.

If you speculate and lose do not continue to speculate in the hope of covering your first loss. This is gambling and a big trap.

On average shares perform well, however as a few may quickly more than double in price a few may also go broke and disappear.

29. Calculating profits

Calculating desired profit eg 10%

$2.00 a share multiplied by 10% = $0.20 + $2.00 = $2.20

$5000 divided by $2.00 = 2500 shares multiplied by $2.20 = $5500.

$5000 - $5500 = $500 in profit

30. Determining share price movement in the short term

You may be able to determine if a share price will rise or fall in the short term by enquiring through a broker on the number of buyers and the price they have set and the number of sellers and the price they have set. For example a share that last traded at $2 has an order to sell 500 shares at $2.10 and 800 other sellers at $2.15 whilst there are 6000 buyers at $1.99. As there are more buyers than sellers you may assume the price could rise. However as shares should be a mostly long term investment this on the day calculation has no effect on the long term outcome. Brokers can also provide lots of other information on companies such as the dividend and the share price high and low for the year.

31. Time in the share market

Good profits can be made by buying at the right time and selling shortly after when the price has risen to a predetermined percentage and then buy another share considered to be at a good price and so on. If this was done over a five year period you may have made a considerable profit, however you may or may not have done better by just keeping the original shares you purchased for five years and by doing so having saved brokerage fees etc.

Some traders believe some shares run in a yearly cycle, starting around November when more people start to purchase shares and peaking around May when they then start to lose a little of their gains. This however would possibly not have a great effect on the overall share prices as the share price is mainly affected by company profits etc.
{Profit is not made until the shares are sold}
Profit's and diversification
You should not sell shares if they are still likely to continue to grow, unless you have picked another that has a better chance of growth or you wish to diversify your investments into other areas or you need the money.

32. Public floats

Some public floats can be a good investment even with small amounts of money $1500 +. There are no brokerage fees to buy shares and many, especially government floats, have done quite well in the short term as well as the long term. For example CBA July 1996 $6.00 and Telstra November 1997 $1.95.

You may not be able to obtain the amount that you applied for as you may only be entitled to a small number and then a percentage of your order which could be a problem. To overcome this you could apply for a higher amount or double the order by purchasing a second lot in your partners name.

You may be able to obtain more shares from a variety of brokers if you are their client, then transfer all the shares to only one broker before selling to minimise brokerage fee on sale. Buy more shares if the price is or becomes reasonable when the float is listed on the ASX (Australia Stock Exchange). Alternatively you may decide to sell if the price rises sharply to a level you consider to be unsustainable. (Percentage of profit to time). Then possibly buy back if the price falls sufficiently.

Not all public floats are good, it pays to research the company.

33. Methods for selecting shares

Past experiments in buying shares have shown some unusual results eg ten shares were picked at random and the results recorded after one year. Ten worst performing shares for the year have also been picked and results recorded the following year. In both cases the results out-perform shares picked by several investment advisers. The reasons being during that time period on average three in every four companies listed performed well. Also luck in selecting the companies and the performances of each group were averaged as no doubt some would have performed poorly.

In the case of the lower performing shares it may have been that a lot of the companies had performed well, but this was not reflected in their share price growth or they had spent money on expansion etc and were showing the profits in the following year or a change in company strategy.

Another method of selecting shares is by using price graphs of companies to compare their performance to see which have performed best over the long term and are showing a little downturn in their present price. This method may be helpful, however the best reason for picking shares is still growth, why and how long accompanied by good figures eg P/E ratio and NTA etc and of course luck still plays a role.

{Missing the falls in the market is not as important as being in the market when it rises}

{Profits can be made by timing the market, but time in the market gives the most profit}

34. The advantages of negative gearing shares, property and taxation

Maximising tax benefit's by using your partner.
If investing in shares or managed fund etc with a partner you may wish to have the investment in the name of the partner who pays the lowest tax to minimise tax pay on the investments. You may need to modify the Will of the partner who has the investment to ensure the investments are returned in case of an accident. See in the property section for advantages of property over shares.

Negative gearing shares
For this you require another source of taxable income (eg wage) and a loan to buy the shares preferably an interest only loan. If you only pay the interest on the loan the whole payments can be claimed as a Tax deduction.

As you do not pay Capital Gains Tax on shares until they are sold you are only profiting at this stage from your dividend payments which should be lower than your interest payments on your loan. You are therefore running at a loss. You use this loss and costs etc. to reduce your tax payable on your second income (eg wage) and possibly receive a tax refund.

Over the long term share prices should have grown substantially. Sell the shares and pay off the capital on the loan and the Capital Gains Tax. You should be left with a nice profit and have paid less tax on your second income. Capital Gains Tax is calculated on profit after inflation divided by 5 and added to your other income to calculate the Tax bracket to be used on your other income plus your Capital Gains after inflation.

Eg sale price $20,000 subtract purchase price $7,000 = $13,000 profit, subtract inflation on purchase price $3,000 = $10,000 divided by 5 = $2,000. Add this $2,000 to your other incomes to calculate which Tax bracket you will now be assessed in. Step 2: This Tax bracket percentage rate is now applied to calculate what tax you owe on the total of your other incomes and the Capital Gains Profit which in this case is $10,000 ($13,000 profit subtract inflation $3,000 = $10,000). Fees and other cost are also subtracted from profit

 (keep all records for 5 years)

(Loan interest rates may suddenly rise dramatically increasing your repayments. You need to have calculated for this and have adequate funds to cover these rises if you intend borrowing or negative gearing.)

If you have owned the shares for more than one year your Capital Gains Tax may be calculated at a lower rate. eg 1/2

There are advantages of negative gearing shares over property. Firstly you haven't got to worry about keeping a tenant. With shares you can also vary the amount of money you wish to borrow. If you get yourself into financial difficulty you can sell some of the shares, but it is hard to sell one part of your property. Property is generally a longer term investment than shares.

Shares over the long term have usually out perform all other investments eg property. As a loan is required for negative gearing shares or properties etc, you are required to make regular payments. This is a forced way of saving for those who find it difficult to form a saving habit but are able to pay their financial commitments.

Capital Gain's Tax (*Not all Countries*)
Apart from dividends, paying tax on shares is only payable on shares after they have been sold at a profit (Capital Gains Tax.) If shares are sold at a loss, the loss can then offset tax owing on profits made on capital gains. Losses can be carried forward indefinitely, however Dividend Earnings that are franked that are not used to pay tax owed can be claimed back again at the end of the financial year in cash as they can't be carried forward to the next financial year.

If your income is below the taxable amount for a set year you could sell shares that have made a profit to bring your income up to the tax threshold. These shares could then be bought straight back at a similar price. Then when you decide to sell your shares in a year where you are above the tax threshold you would only be paying tax owed on the second purchase, not the full amount of growth since the initial purchase.

35. Low inflation and or interest rates

Low **Inflation** is good for share investment because it usually means companies and their customers have low interest payments on their loan's which helps company profits. High Inflation may be an advantage to property investors if it increases property prices more than the effects on the cost. Other things may affect share and property prices such as the state of the economy, performance and value, demand and the jumping on the band wagon rush in fear of missing out. These are some of the factors that can make some shares and properties become over or under valued.

36. Managed funds or super funds

Managed funds or trust accounts are another good form of investment. For example Money Market which invests mainly in fixed interest and cash. The following investments put their money in a variety of areas depending on the amount of profit and risk desired. Generally speaking the greater the profit the greater the risk. Capital Secure, Capital Stable and Managed all invest in a variety of the following areas. Fixed interest, cash, bonds, property, Australian Shares and International shares **{Equity Trusts}**. Specialised funds may invest in mainly one area. For example a Property portfolio, Australian Share portfolio and International share portfolio etc. International share portfolios are also affected by the value of the Australian dollar (exchange rates). A lower dollar when you are selling would increase your profits.

Make sure your fund manager is a member of the FPA (Financial Planning Association) or IAFP (International Association for Financial Planning)

Some investment advisers may only recommend funds that pay them a commission. Fees for managed funds vary. Usually those that give higher returns require more management and have higher fees. The types of fees may vary from one of or a mixture of the following entry, ongoing, switching and exit fees. A particular fund may have two options, entry fee or nil entry fee. The entry fee fund has either a lower ongoing fee or pays a higher interest. Generally you are better off with an entry fee fund if you intend to stay in for longer than 4 years.

For example entry fee 4%, with an ongoing fee 1%, or a nil entry fee with an ongoing fee 2% or the fund pays a slightly smaller amount of interest. Some fund advisers will recommend you only deal with the one company to eliminate duplication of fees. However as a lot of funds work on a percentage basis eg 4% in 1% ongoing, it makes little difference as to whether you have one fund or five as the fees are not a set amount, but a percentage of your money invested.

Therefore a little diversification may be safer. (Note some funds also have set fees. If these are too high then diversification may be costly, always keep an eye on the fees).

Some funds claim to have no fees. They can do this by having a buy price higher than the sell price, eg a $1.04 to buy a unit at that time and $1 if selling the same unit at that time which is a 4% difference. These funds may also pay a slightly lower interest rate say 1% lower which would be equivalent to the ongoing fee. You could almost say you are still paying a 4% entry fee and a 1% ongoing fee.

Discount brokers also deal in Managed Funds and offer a substantially cheaper entry fees for some Managed Funds. Each financial year the Managed Funds will send you a letter telling you how much the funds have made (income) and how much Tax you owe. If however you buy your own shares you are taxed on the capital growth only when you sell them.

A Managed Fund maybe a good investment if you don't have enough money to adequately spread your investments into enough different shares to give a good diversity. A managed fund in Shares and or Property should give you diversity.

Dealing through a normal broker or a discount broker for shares or managed fund investments. For managed funds a discount broker may only charge 1% as compared to 4 - 5% entry fee and ongoing fee of 1% by a non-discount broker. However the non-discount broker should help you with an investment strategy and save you time in researching and possibly provide you with better investments. Some brokers will only deal with certain fund managers. If you make your own choices you may have a wider range to choose from and as you are paying less in fees you have more to invest and if your selections are good you will receive more profits. Super Fund and non-super Managed Fund: Super funds may have good tax advantages but are usually not accessible until retirement age, non-super Managed Funds are usually accessible but have no tax advantages.

37. Time and risk when investing

Time and risk

If you are investing in a Managed Fund or Super Fund and plan to invest for a long time, say fifteen years, you may choose a fund with a higher return and a higher risk (International Shares, Australian Share, Property). If after ten years the fund has performed well and there is no or only a small switching fee you may be wiser to switch 70% of the fund to a safer fund (Cash) for the last five years. This will ensure you still have a good return if the more volatile fund falls at the time you wish to withdraw.

38. Investing in property

Properties can also be negatively geared.

Things to look for are:

- Location and location!
- How long has it taken for properties to double in value in that area?
- Would you like to live in it?
- Would it suit renting out?
- Would it have good resale value?
- {Obtain a copy of a independent evaluation and the lenders evaluation because if you use your home as collateral worth say $300,000 and say you only owe $20,000 on it, your new property may be worth $400,000 so the lender may lend you up to $600,000 for your new property}
- Find out if the property you are purchasing is not too expensive and the other houses in the area or street are of equal or greater value as this would tend to increase the value of your property.
- The land size, could it be subdivided for a unit by you or the next owner and if so would there be independent access to the new units or house.

- Does the area have good employment possibilities and good population growth?

- Close to facilities eg shops, schools, public transport and city centre.

- Is it closely located near a popular natural feature such as a beach etc. as this maybe an excellent buying point.

- Natural features are less likely to change as other things in the area might such as employment prospects.

- New Major Road and or transport developments in the area may help the property rise in value.

- (Is there suitable employment for you and are there leisure activities in the area that suit you?)

- Is the property low maintenance eg brick, aluminium windows etc.

- For reasonable costs can it be improved to increase the value eg build garage, build fences, build low maintenance gardens maybe try not to spend more than 10% of the property value. Of course this can vary dramatically either way depending on the realistic value the improvement will generate in saving future costs of maintenance, increased rent or property value. If these would not be achieved by making improvements, then perhaps there is no need to make improvements. You would possibly expect to spend on a property you are going to renovate and sell for a quick profit; however a property you are going to negative gear to rent you may want to keep costs more to a minimum and only spend on those things that can realistically increase rent and or property value and possibly be claimed as a tax deduction.

- A good appearance to the front of the house eg gardens and paths should add value, neat and tidy back yard, neat garage, modern bathroom / kitchen should add value however bbq's, pools are trends and may not have value.

- Be careful not to waste money on improvements that won't add value to your property {Making a Renovators Business Card may help you to obtain a trade discount on materials}. Remember though you most likely won't want a property that needs too much work doing as this is a cost even though in some cases it may greatly increase the value of the property, you may not be able to rent it while you are doing repairs and therefore you may not be able to claim repairs as a cost on the rental income.

- Check with Councils to see if there is likely to be any developments in the area that will affect the property.

- Has the property got a nice view?

- Is the property located and designed in such a manner that it will not become too hot or cold when the seasons change (sunlight blocked, foggy area)

- Is the property likely to be too boggy in the winter months due to rain or underground springs?

- You should have the property inspected by a registered and qualified builder or building inspector for structural soundness and possible future expenses, wiring, plumbing, termites and borers. (You need to be very careful when selecting an inspector as if they do not do a thorough job and you realise your property is termite riddled after say 3 months and the inspector says prove they were there when I inspected the place, you may have difficulties.)

- Has the property been built in an area that was previously exposed to chemicals such as an old tip site?

- Is the area prone to flooding **or storm damage,** (do you consider the theory sea levels may rise 8 metres).

- Noise levels in the area. Some noise levels may only occur at certain times of the year eg race tracks or speed ways.

(You should pick a property that has the most chance of **growing in value**.) {Select tenants just as carefully. Ask them to provide references, current credit check, proof of the time period they have been using their current name and proof of their ability to meet the rent requirements. You should also use an appropriate lease agreement.} Property is generally a longer term investment than shares. Investing in an inner city unit can also be a good investment. When you sell your investment property you may need to pay Capital Gains Tax which is calculated on profit after inflation. You may however not have to pay Capital Gains Tax if you have lived in the property for a certain period of time.

Working out what you should pay for an investment property. Look at the value of rents in the area. They may vary from $200 - $500 per week, however the main bulk may be paying around $300. You may want a property a little more upmarket and therefore decide $350 is the rent that you would desire to charge and in the area you are in there are still a reasonable amount of people who can afford this rent for a house a little above average. Take your weekly desired rent, multiply it by 52, which is your yearly rental income, work this out as a percentage of the value of the house you are looking at purchasing and this may be say 6% return. This means the house you are looking at purchasing to achieve this would cost around $303,333 (350x52/0.06). A property over this value you may have to charge more rent for which you may not achieve in your area. Some of the reasons you may be paying slightly above average for your rental property may be because it is a little more modern and requires less maintenance, plus a little more desirable to rent or own. Of course the 6% return is not accurate because it does not cover costs; the real return also counts the growth in property value and growth in rent over time.

Some of the advantages of negatively gearing property over shares are the interest rates on the loans maybe cheaper for property and more deductions can usually be claimed on properties to cut the amount of tax you are paying on your income. Examples of claims; interest on loan, maintenance of property, inspection trips to the property, insurances also include rental income insurance, management fees, rates, Building and Fittings Depreciation depending on age, etc. It may not be possible to claim most of these costs unless the property was being rented at the time the costs were incurred. Depreciation on property can be claimed if the property is not older than 40 years. Therefore the newer the property the better.

A possible reason that there may be more tax incentives for property than shares is that the government sometimes likes to encourage the building of new properties to assist in the boosting of the economy and also to ensure that adequate rental properties are available as this can also slightly reduce the need on government housing properties.

One theory in property investing is never to sell. Obtain an interest only loan to purchase a $300,000 property. When this property rises in value (equity) use this equity to purchase another property and so on to build a large portfolio of properties. You may have purchased $1,000,000 worth of property, but after 10 years they are worth $2,200,000. You still owe around $1,000,000, but you now have equity of around $1,200,000. You may also have an overdraft account (line of credit) to pay things like rates, insurances etc where you have only been paying off the interest and this may mean you also owe $20,000 on this account therefore your equity is now around $1,180,000. When you retire don't live off the rent and don't sell. Just borrow on your equity as you need to, but this time not to purchase more properties, rather to retire on. This way your not paying capital gains tax and you still have your properties which hopefully are still growing in value over the next 10 years.

However to meet bank and taxation requirements you may need to say you are living off your rental income and your new loan is to meet the shortfall in payments on your old loans as a consequence of you now living off your rental income as some loans need to be for something that has the potential of making a profit.

Of course this scenario depends on interest rates and properties rising favourably. Usually however these do work in favour of the investor.

There are a lot of schemes that involve borrowing or borrowing on your equity (assets). Some may make you very rich, some may also do the same but only in the short term. You need to be adequately prepared for the downturn in the cycle and able to last until the upturn returns and also realise some of the schemes could eventually send you broke.

Always search around for incentive deals offered by institutions and governments eg good interest rates, bonuses for achieving targets, grants etc eg a government scheme may offer for a home loan $50,000 interest free with no need to pay back the $50,000 for 15 years. This of course would save you a huge amount in interest payments and possibly allow you to utilise this money elsewhere, maybe in a low risk secure investment with reasonable returns. With any such scheme it is important to always check the conditions and fine print, but the point is it can be worthwhile contacting different institutions and government bodies to see what is on offer as some grants and incentives etc are not always well promoted.

{The value of a property = the cost of building the house - $1000 for each year the house has aged + the current value of the land. This indicates that the growth in land value in the area you chose is important. and/or Property Value P = Annual Rent R / Average Growth G in property value in %. eg $200,000 = $8400 / 7%

$P = R / G$, $R = P * G$, $G = R / P$. NOTE these formulas are not always totally accurate or reliable.}

{Unique Features that are in demand assist in selling and renting eg view, water frontages}

(Loan interest rates may suddenly rise dramatically increasing your repayments. You need to have calculated for this and have adequate funds to cover these rises if you intend borrowing or negative gearing.)

{The greater the population growth in the area you buy your property, the better your chance's of growth in your property value.}

Perhaps you could consider buying a property to live in a few years before you need to reside in it and rent it until this time arises. This may give you a head start on owning your own property.

Positive Gearing means you are making a profit after paying expenses. You can still claim expenses on your tax but will possibly pay tax on your profit. Your assets should grow in value and you are making money along the way. To Positive Gear a property you may need the annual rent to be about 10% of the property value and or (loan amount). Weekly rent * 52 * 10 = property value or property value * 0.1 / 52 = Weekly rent. (or Shares that pay around a 7.7% full franked dividends 7.7% * 1.3% = 10% a smaller dividend may be adequate if a deposit is paid.)

Neutral Gearing means your cost equal your expenses you pay no tax and make no money along the way and your assets should grow in value.

When you sell you may need to pay capital gains tax.

You can also vary the size of your deposit to determine whether you are Negative Gearing, Positive Gearing or Neutral Gearing in either property or shares.

Some people believe you need to borrow money to really make money. You borrow for a business, investment properties or shares. This can be true if you invest wisely, carefully manage your investments and the economy runs in favour of your investments and you may do extremely well. However if you are unlucky and or the economy runs badly for your investment and or you have employment problems you may have difficulty in paying your loan.

Some investment advisers like the idea of you borrowing large amounts of money for their investment ideas as it also gives you lots of money to pay their fees. If you borrow a $100,000 and make $25,000 could you borrow $300,000 and make $75,000?? or risk losing a larger amount.

{The Idea of investing is to enjoy the outcome but make sure you also enjoy the journey}

{In Business some people are mainly interested in your money and what they tell you may not exactly be the truth, more likely its what They want you to know or what You want to hear, neither maybe realistic. Always spend the necessary time to research and consider important or costly decisions}

39. Differences in property loans

A loan that is paid monthly in amounts of $400 compared to a loan that is paid off fortnightly at $200. The $400 would be paid 12 times in the year which equals $4800. The $200 would be paid 26 times in the year which equals $5200, the fortnightly having one extra payment. This extra payment over time would save a considerable amount and reduce the time period of the loan. However more importantly the interest rates are calculated daily so due to this paying fortnightly over time will have a greater effect on reducing your loan. Also using a mortgage offset account can assist in reducing the amount of loan repayments (see blow).

Things to look for in loans are:

- It may be beneficial to have separate loans, eg one for the property you reside in and other separate loans for your investment properties so as if you need to refinance one investment property or sell one investment property you are not hassled having to do a total refinance.
- Having a flexible loan that has favourable fees eg no penalties for early termination of the loan.
- A loan that will allow extra payments to be made and calculates the interest owed on a regular basis eg weekly or daily so as extra payments will reduce interest owed more quickly.
- Does the lending institute have a good rating (Mooneys triple A)
- Will the loan allow you to borrow extra money for extensions etc.
- Can the loan be transferred to another home at a later time.

These are all features to look for in a loan as well as a competitive interest rate. Beware some loans have a honeymoon rate which has a good low interest rate only given for the first year. By paying extra payments or increasing your payments by $5 or $10 will in the long term often save years and thousands of dollars in the repayments. You should check whether the extra payments are going towards paying off the capital or the interest. The more that pays off the capital the better.

A badly planned loan with a small deposit, high interest rates or rising interest rates and inadequate repayments may find the payments are not even covering the accruing interest therefore the amount owed would be increasing. On the other hand a well planned affordable loan with a good deposit and extra payments may significantly reduce the time in years it takes to pay off the loan and also reduce the total amount paid by thousands.

Two loans both at $45,000 at 8%, the first one with a $5000 deposit and fortnightly repayments of $240 and the second one with a $8000 deposit and fortnightly repayments of $265. The first loan would take 9 years to pay back at a total of $56,000 and the second loan would take 7 years to pay back at a total of $48,000. This is a saving of 3 years and $8,000. Due to the relatively high interest on loans the bigger the deposit or extra payments or adding to payments to reduce the time on the loan and the amount owed is definitely worth while.

If a one year loan is extended to two years you roughly double the interest you pay but nearly halve your payments. If you continue to increase the loans pay period the payments will continue to decrease but not as significantly as the interest begins to rapidly increase until the point where increasing the time period will begin to increase the payments. A loan needs to have affordable payments over time with the interest being not to extreme.

An Equity Loan works on the principle your whole pay goes straight into your housing loan. You then operate from monthly accounts and your credit card, the type that sends you the bill at the end of the month and then allows you one month to pay, charging you no interest providing you fully pay by the end of that month. You then pay this by drawing money from your equity loan to do so. This means that you have had extra money in your account for two months which in turn would have reduced the interest you owe. Also if you have reduced your spending you would have left extra money in the account to pay off your loan.

The problem with these loans is as you are mainly using a credit card if you are not good at budgeting you could easily spend more than you have allocated and leave inadequate funds to cover your loan payments thus increasing your interest and/or the time it takes you to pay off the loan.

Mortgage Offset Account or Redraw Facility: Your loan is at 8% and you also have $10,000 for emergencies or investing that you can invest at 6%. If you instead place the $10,000 in your Mortgage Offset Account you would save paying 8% on $10,000 of your mortgage which makes you 2% better off than you would have been if you had of invested the $10,000 at 6%. You are allowed to redraw part or all off the $10,000 when you need it. You could also look at having the weekly rent you collect paid directly into your mortgage offset account.

Using an overdraft facility to buy share's rather than a straight loan. If you had say a $100,000 overdraft you still pay fees the same as a loan, but you're only paying interest on the money that you have used to buy shares not the whole amount of the overdraft limit. This means you can take a little more time to select your shares or if you need to reduce the amount of interest you are paying you could sell a few shares to reduce the amount drawn from your overdraft limit. Fees and interest charges should be tax deductible and you may wish to use your dividend payments to help with the interest payments. If your shares perform well this may prove to be a profitable and flexible investment opportunity. If they do not perform well you need to be able to still afford the interest payment fees and cover the losses.

Therefore as with any loan or investment decision the figures need to be looked at carefully, the possible benefits and the amount of risk you are prepared to take. It would not be advisable to use an overdraft and or a loan for shares until you have had at least three years experience in the share market with at least a quarter of the amount of the money you would use. An overdraft facility would probably not suit a property investment.

40. The home you live in

The home you live in (if you are buying) is not necessarily an investment. The costs related to it are a financial liability. Rent is also a financial liability. The question is, by renting can you (and will) you save more in the time it takes to pay off the house than the house will be worth at this time (payments plus interest plus, cost insurance, rates, maintenance or saving plus interest earned less rent). The next question is where will you be the happiest, in your own house where you have a little more control or a rental property where you have less responsibility and are able to move easier. How quick can you pay of a loan or how good can you save. Rent Assistance can be obtained if your assets and income are below the limits set, but similar assistance can not be obtain if you reside in a house you are buying.

    Renting a $300,000 house 4% $12,000/52= $231 a week rent.
    Buying a $300,000 house 7% $18,000/52= $346 a week bank interest.

Strata Lease is buying a home at a reduced price thus having more money to invest or spend. You can not resell or give away the strata lease home as the ownership converts back to the original owner when you leave.

A question of lifestyle...Your home should enhance your lifestyle without over extending your finances so as to inhibit your lifestyle. Balance enjoying life now and going without to plan for the future.

You don't want to go into debt or an investment that will affect your sleep and therefore your health. You don't want to need to work to the extent that it will reduce your spare time required for keeping fit and enjoying life.

More important than a good deposit is an affordable loan. It is no good having a big deposit if the loan payments are not affordable to you.

Insurance: may not cover you for everything eg all natural disasters, termites, arson and if you are on holiday and your house is vacant for a period of time eg over four weeks it may not be covered. It is important that you make sure your insurance meets your needs and you are not under or over insured

{If you have only one choice you'll probably take it. If you are lucky? and have three to choose from, you may find it difficult to make any choice}

You need to work out the type of investment strategy that suits you. This may depend on your lifestyle, debts you need to service, capital you have available, how much you are able to save and risks that you are prepared to take, employment security, responsibilities you have etc.
1) You may just decide to go with a good budget at first to reduce debt.
2) Or you may be able to budget and start up a small bonus savings account that pays reasonable interest.
3) You may wish to pay your house off and open a managed fund account which requires minimal time and risk on your behalf.
4) You may wish to try for higher gains over a longer term and spend more time researching your investment and managing your investment by selecting your own shares or purchasing rental properties. You may also need to work out when you are doing this if you are better off paying off your own home or renting.
It is a good idea, no matter which choice you choose, to gain advice off an experienced and licensed investment adviser and write down your goals, how you are going to achieve them and the time frame you would like to achieve your goals. Also perhaps include best and worst case scenarios and steps you may put in place to reduce worst case scenarios and increase the chances of achieving best case scenarios.

If you needed to borrow $5000 and you have the option of a personal loan at 10% or extending to your home loan which is at only 5% you may actually be better with the personal loan as if you were required to pay this off within a year you would pay approximately $500 interest whereas if you paid it off over 3 years using the home loan as it is 5% per year you may end up paying around $700 interest. However if you are able to put the extra $5000 back into your home loan within the year, then the home loan would remain the better option so you must always consider the interest rate as well as the time frame.

Home Loan

1. What rating has the company got e.g. Mooney's triple A ?
2. Is there a lower interest rate for the first year (Honeymoon rate)?
What is the rate?
3. What is the current variable interest rate?
4. What is the fixed interest rate?
For how many years is it fixed?
5. Do you lend 100% of evaluation?
If not what percentage % ?
6. What is the minimum deposit required?
7. Can payments be made weekly or fortnightly?
What are payments?
8. When is interest calculated, daily, weekly, fortnightly or monthly?
9. How is payment made?
10. When is payment taken from nominated account daily, weekly, fortnightly or monthly?
11. Can weekly or fortnightly payments be increased or decreased?
12. Can extra lump sum payments be made (Mortgage Offset Account)?
If there is a minimum lump sum amount payable what is it?
Is it taken off the capital, interest or both?
13. Can extra money be borrowed for extensions, renovations, car loan, etc (Mortgage Offset Account) or (Redraw Facilitate)? {Note borrowing extra money may not necessarily be a good idea}
14. What are the entry fees, exit fees, Government charges and are there any yearly or on going fees or costs?
15. Are there any early termination fees or penalties for paying the loan of earlier?
16. Can the loan be transferred to another home at a later time?

17. You'll most likely have the choice between a fixed or variable loan and be required to sign a contract once you have made your choice. However if for some reason two years down the track circumstances change and you decide you are better with the other and your contract has a five year penalty clause for changing, you may then find you incur heavy fees and penalties. You may initially be able to negotiate these fees before signing a contract in case you do change your mind or negotiate a shorter time period. If you cannot it is important to think carefully before signing in case your circumstances do change. Be aware of these factors and unfortunately you can't always predict circumstances and get it right. Similar penalties and time frames may also occur if you decide to change to another lender or the term of the loan. After considering the fees and penalty costs it may still be worth the effort of changing.

18. What type of insurance is required and can any company be used?

19. What is their method of debt collecting?

20. Will a marriage split affect your ability to pay the loan?

21. How secure is your income?

Turnover Income & Profit:

Person X buys a bottle of wine for $10 and sells it for $30.

Person Y buys a bottle of wine for $45 and sells it for $50.

Person X has a turnover of $40, income of $30, cost of $10 and a profit or earnings of $20.

Person Y has a turnover of $95, income of $50, cost of $45 and a profit or earnings of $5.

{Note a higher turnover and or income does not necessarily mean higher profits, people forget costs and do not often record all their costs}

Tax Rate: (*Not all Countries*)

Person (A) is in the 30 cent tax rate earning $35,000. Tax paid is $2380 for the first $20,000 plus 30 cents in each $ of $15,000 = $4,500. A total of $6,880, which is 19.66% of the $35,000. Taking home $28,120

Person (B) is in the 30 cent tax rate earning $49,000 Tax paid is $2380 for the first $20,000 plus 30 cents in each $ of $29,000 = $8,700. A total of $11,080 which is 22.61% of the $49,000. Taking home $37,920

Person (C) is in the 42 cent tax rate earning $51,000 Tax paid is $11380 for the first $50,000 plus 42 cents in each $ of $1,000 = $420. A total of $11,800 which is 23.14% of the $51,000. Taking home $39,200

Person A and B were on the 30 cent rate but one paid 19.66% and the other paid 22.61%. Person C was on the 42 cent and paid 23.14% a little more than person B.

Tax did not suddenly jump 12% from 30% to 42% on every dollar earned.

Conclusion: The amount of tax you pay does not suddenly increase when you hit the next tax bracket, rather it slowly increases as your earnings increase. Perhaps the worry is not what tax bracket you are in, but how much you want to earn and how much time do you need for leisure?

Person B 30 cent tax rate earning $49,000. $2380 for the first $20,000 / $2380 = 11.9%. 30% of* $29,000 = $8,700. $8700 + $2380 = $11,080. $11080 / $49,000 = 22.61%. $49,000 - $11,080 = $37,920 Taking home.

(The above calculation does not consider the 1.5% medicare levy etc. etc. nor involve methods of reducing tax to lower the initial income.)

41. Crypto currency

The current top six crypto currencies are: BTC Bitcoin, ETH Ethereum, XRP Ripple, BCH Bitcoin Cash, EOS EOS, LTC Litecoin.

I am not qualified to give advice in any way in this area, but heres my thoughts on the pros and cons. Crypto currency is most likely here to stay. There appears to be big gains to be made here, but also the possibility of big losses. Digital currency of one kind or another has been with us for a long time. Things like tap and go, paypal, electronic transfers, credit cards are all a type of digital currency and more uses for this type of currency are being developed every day and are becoming more popular.

Some time ago a small number of IT professionals were toying with getting rid of money and having an international currency, eliminating bank and government fees. Its development faded away until the USA stock market crash. Now bitcoin exists. This has opened up another way of transferring funds around the world including to countries where in the past one may have had more of a reliance on companies like western union which may have charged a hefty fee. Bitcoin did have about 2% - 4% of its transactions on the Silk Road, but this has since been reigned in by authorities.

One way to store your crypto currency is to purchase an electronic wallet. These look similar to a USB stick and cost around $150. To buy crypto currency you can locate a reputable online seller, submit a few documents to prove your identification and transfer your funds across. They then purchase the crypto currency and the transaction is sent to your electronic wallet where the crypto currency is stored. You are also given a code to enable you to open your wallet and view your crypto currency.

Some companies have installed ATM's in point of sale venues. They can usually accept 2 – 6 types of crypto currencies like bitcoin, bitcoin cash and ethereum meaning you can use their machines to buy or convert these crypto currencies into cash. There are also apps that allow you to store your crypto currency on your mobile device. You can then make purchases in stores that also have the software applications available. So for example in the USA you can by coffee at starbucks with bitcoin.

Your phone displays your bitcoin barcode and the amount you have in bitcoin, they then scan the barcode and your total drops. Another example, in a restaurant you scan a QR label and then select pay and they receive your payment.

There still seems to be growth in companies accepting bitcoin and the like for transactions so over time more local shops will most likely start accepting crypto currency along with online sellers. Some organisations even allow you to have part of your pay converted to crypto currency.

With crypto currency the worries of some countries printing too much money or economies crashing or currency conversions / bank fees etc are reduced somewhat. This makes it popular with travellers and tourists and those regularly sending money to other countries. Security with bitcoin is supposedly as good as or better than a bank, however if banks do become compromised and your assets are negatively affected the banks usually guarantee your assets and eventually reinstate your finances. The nature of crypto currencies using the block chain technology makes them virtually unhackable, but you'd want to make sure you're buying from a reputable seller and not misplace your access to your electronic wallet.

Crypto currency predominantly gets its security by using block chain technology. Block chain technology works by using thousands of computers around the world to keep the records of transactions and by cross referencing this information. This therefore should mean that your crypto currency is more secure as hackers would need to be able to hack all these computers simultaneously. Mining crypto currency; you can become a part of this block chain by allowing your computer to be used and in return for this you are given a small amount of crypto currency. To improve you ability to mine crypto currency there are specialised computers available usually fitted with high performance graphics cards. Mining would also be affected by your internet connection and speed.

To see if this would be worthwhile for you, you would need to be able to work out what you can make less the cost of your equipment and power costs etc to run this equipment 24/7, so on a small scale it might not provide much income at all.

Some are investing in bitcoin and other crypto currency in the hope of continued growth. Banks appear to be making changes to compete, with features such as tap and go. The USA are now regulating bitcoin more making those that start up bitcoin businesses have to show liquidity. Of course the original bitcoin founders were trying to avoid such regulations and government controls. Some countries may look at banning bitcoin and other crypto currency, but it doesn't look like the USA will do that considering they are putting in regulations and a lot of companies in the UK, USA and Europe are now accepting bitcoin.

Whilst crypto currency itself at this stage seems to avoid government taxes and fees, some of those that provide the change from hard currency to the virtual currency want a hefty fee for doing so, some up to 10%, thus this half defeats the purpose. However there are other ways of obtaining bitcoin for example that don't involve fees or huge fees. The usual fee for buying bitcoin or other crypto currency is currently around 1% – 3%. Some times you can sell or swap to an alternate coin for no fee, however like with everything the companies who do the trading in crypto currency and converting cash into crypto currency are the ones who will likely profit the most from the crypto market.

The idea of course is it's a more stable currency, more universally accepted which minimises fees and taxes. Since around 2017 bitcoin seems to have gone from $4000 up to $25000 then dropping to around $10000 all within a 12 month period. Like some other investments crypto currency has had its moments where it's rallied out of control and then dropped off. It may now settle for a little while before having another run, but this looks like an investment that may be a little prone to dramatic price raises and falls along the way.

Bitcoin has been around for a good seven years however crypto currencies in general are probably still in their early stages of gaining a foothold on becoming more mainstream.

Another unique thing of bitcoin is they only released a set number of bitcoin. So unlike a country when your population doubles and the government prints more money, with bitcoin as the demand for it increases so the price and value of it should increase. As bitcoin may be worth $10K a coin so eventually your 0.0004 cup of coffee may cost 0.0002 if the demand eventually doubles the price of the bitcoin. Due to the high cost of bitcoin now, it is quite normal not to buy a whole bitcoin, but a bit of a bitcoin eg you could buy just $200 worth of bitcoin. The price can also increase and decrease upon fear and greed. This may be the downside of bitcoin because it could become largely overvalued due to greed rather than demand on usage and therefore also vulnerable to panic and a great decrease making it more like investing in speculative shares in the short term. Demand one would think should see the price continue to rise perhaps, as the number of bitcoin does not increase, but what if its use is banned by a large number of countries? Will it be replaced by an alternative or will the banks catch up and offer better?

Some people are developing their own crypto currency to raise money for a business idea. This would be similar to forming a company and floating it on the share market. Creating ones own crypto currency may possibly make it easier to obtain funds, but many of these businesses will fail and only some will succeed. For example a transport company is using block chain technology to enable it and its customers to track its shipments thus making the company more efficient and offering a secure tracking method for its customers. If the company becomes profitable then the coin they are using becomes popular and the price should rise. The possible disadvantage of crypto currency is however with the increasing number and types of coins becoming available.

For example with a coin like bitcoin the number of coins produced is limited and with popularity these two factors should lead to the coin rising in price due to its limited supply. However as the more types of coins become available this actually increases the supply of crypto currencies in general and it is likely therefore not all crypto currencies will be viable.

It is inevitable that crypto currencies are here to stay in some form or another as the advantages of electronic money takes hold and becomes more commonly used. It's just a question of which currencies will do well and which will disappear.

42. Savings for your children

You could consider opening a super account for your children. First you need to apply for a tax file number, and then you could maybe deposit one or two thousand dollars. This then establishes a nice amount in the super that should gain interest and not be eaten away by fees. It also establishes a super under the current laws so if changes in laws take place like retirement ages etc you then sometimes have the choice of which rules to go under. The children may also be eligible for government incentives such as super co contributions, however to achieve this they would need to earn a recognised small amount of money from possibly something like a pamphlet round and this employment would need to be their main source of income which if is their only form of income would not need to be much. You would need to check you comply with other relevant rules. Because the super has been started at an early age the interest gained on the initial small deposit would be quite substantial. The disadvantage is of course the money becomes locked up for a long time.

Another investment you could consider for your children would perhaps be buying a parcel of shares in trust to your children say around $3000 in a blue chip company like a bank.

However to avoid possibly having to fill out a tax form for your children you may need to purchase shares that do not pay a dividend or shares that offer dividend reinvest but are not franked as any shares that offer franking you will need to fill out a tax form to claim back the franking credits. Whilst the money from the franking credits is placed in the child's bank account you will have had to have completed a small tax form to do this each year, but where there are no credits paid hopefully the portfolio increase over time and you will not be required to fill out a tax form unless the shares are sold. When they reach say the age of 17 and maybe with a couple of parcels of shares they can then decide whether they will collect the dividends as cash and start filling in tax forms and using the dividends to help with the cost of living.

They also have the choice of using the shares to increase their income via dividends or sell them to help with perhaps a purchase of a car etc which becomes an introduction to budgeting because in a sense you can't have your cake and eat it too. You need to weigh up the facts of a bigger loan or less income and of course you need some income to pay for the running costs of the car and you are usually better to borrow less as interest on loans usually outweigh interest earned. Another advantage of buying shares is you yourself could re-access this money for an emergency or maybe educational needs if circumstances change.

There are also some good children's savings accounts which offer bonus interest. This may also be a good way to teach them to save up over 4 – 12 months for something they want.

Why do scams work? 15% interest guaranteed, double your money. You can be a little vulnerable to these schemes if a previous investment has not done well and you are trying to recoup your losses quickly, but in a lot of cases scams rely on the human nature of greed. Whilst in some cases a lot of unbelievable results can be achieved often if it sounds too good to be true it is too good to be true, so take time to think and do your research and don't fall for the get in quick or miss out spin.

42. Wills

If you jointly own something you can not Will your share to someone because when you pass your share automatically belongs to the other joint owner. If you wish to be able to Will your share to someone else you need to have a legal agreement (deed of tenants in common) stating your share will belong to your estate.

Assets

Who owns them. For taxation purposes income earning assets maybe better off being owned by the lowest income earner. For Centrelink Part B family payment which is paid according to the income of the lowest income earner, therefore if you are eligible the highest earner is better off owning the assets if they are income earning assets.

A person that is in a position or job where they are liable to be sued maybe better off not owning assets.

Maybe the assets should be owned according to the amount of work and capital each person involved has contributed.

Enduring Power Of Attorney

Allows the person or persons you appointed to access your assets for your benefit if you are unable to due to ill health. This power ceases if your health recovers or if you pass away your Will takes over.

Financial Decision

Be careful not to make big irreversible financial decisions or other such decisions when under emotional pressure, take a little extra time to consider the long term effects and real needs.

Retiring and or changing lifestyles: Maybe you'd like to purchase a caravan or boat. Sometimes these lifestyle changes do not work out so perhaps it might be an idea to rent for a period of time to trial the lifestyle change.

Moving house or sea change: It might also be better not to move more than 10km away from where you have been residing as you know the services available in this area and have contacts and friends. Whereas if you move further away and find the area you originally lived in did have certain appeal there may be significant losses that occurred if it decide to sell and move back to the original area. Sometimes a little bit of something is good, but when you can access it all the time the novelty wears off so maybe the occasional holiday is the way to go.

43. Tax

Methods of reducing tax: (*Not all Countries*)

Expense for maintenance and repairs etc. Depreciation of items over $1000 that lose value eg computer. Capital loss on a sale of an item (this only gives a tax credit). Money earned from a hobby is tax free. Hobbies are not time consuming and not the main source of income and are not advertised. Some Business can be changed to a hobby and vice versa.

Sole Trader: A sole trader can employ people, he/she bears all the responsibility and pays all the tax.

Partnership: A partnership can be made with a verbal agreement and the profits can be split to reduce total tax paid. Taxation department must be notified of the percentage of split of each partner at the beginning of each financial year. All partners have the responsibility of liability, but liability may only be sought from the partner who has the easiest to obtain assets.

Companies: Companies can be formed by trustees. The company may only be valued at a few dollars plus assets if any. Due to this financial institutions usually require personal guarantees from each trustee for bank credits and loans.

Always keep receipts. Perhaps you could staple them to the instruction book when appropriate and/or file them. They may come in handy to help keep track of expenses and useful for warranty purposes and Tax.

Self managed superannuation. This does require some set up fees and you do need some knowledge and the time to manage your funds, but as well as being able to select your own shares you can also include property. If you were to place your investment properties at some time into your self managed superannuation at retirement age you may avoid paying some or all capital gains tax.

Disclaimer: This is a learning tool and not professional advice. **Always** seek professional advice before making financial decisions. Before making any decisions information should be checked for changes in policies and accuracy as the information provided cannot be guaranteed. The author will not be liable in any way for any actions taken or not taken by the reader or for any negligent misstatements, errors or omissions. This information is not intended for the use of any third party. No person, persons or organisation should invest monies or take other action on reliance of the material provided, but instead should satisfy themselves independently (whether by expert advice or otherwise) of the appropriateness of any such action.

ShareWhiz [TM]

ShareMaster [TM]

CamperWhiz [TM]

© 2002 - 2018 G.Alex

☺

Table of Contents

- The share market	- Don't speculate
- Percentage of profit to time	- Time in the market
- Selling or buy orders	- Public floats
- Performance example	- Methods for selecting shares
- Discounts	- Negative gearing shares
- Auto-stock loss	- Managed funds
- Blue chip shares	- Time and risk
- Chess system	- Investing in property
- Diversification	- Negatively gearing property
- Quick profits	- Positive gearing
- Spare cash	- Neutral gearing
- Dividends	- Property loans
- Dividend reinvest	- Mortgage offset account
- Formulas	- Home you live in
- Market capitalisation	- Crypto currency
- P/E ratio	- Block chain technology
- NTA	- Budgeting
- Bull and bear	- Superannuation
- Compounding interest	- Annuities or pensions
- Paying out loans	- Turnover income and profit
- Five reasons for investing in shares	- Tax rate
- Researching	- Reducing tax
- Ten tips	- GST tax
- Mining companies	- Wills
- Don't speculate	- Power of attorney
	- Share Whiz™